Here We Begin

Adrian J. Atwater

Copyright © 2020 by Adrian J. Atwater

All rights reserved. This book or any portion thereof may not be reproduced or used in any manner whatsoever, without the express written permission of the publisher except for the use of brief excerpts for a book review, scholarly journal, or via social media platform.

Here We Begin	1
These Moments	4
Bring Hope	6
Know Love	30
Value Peace	60

These Moments

Here We Begin is inspired by the belief that life is like a mosaic, comprised of priceless, countless, granular moments. These moments are the best of us, the worst of us, and how we choose to know them, will eventually come to define us.

I believe we have a right to seek clarity in these moments and use the power of choice to impress upon them. It's our mutual fate, our universal purpose, and I would argue — it's inevitable. Indeed, even when we choose not to choose, we choose to defer. Thus, in honor of our right to ultimately decide, I think it's our responsibility to actively shape the fate of these moments as best we can.

In other words, *Here We Begin* is about self-determination. It's about intentionality as both a cure for complacency and as a basic duty we share. It's about exploring the theory that we're each accountable for causing our own growth. We're each liable to others, for the betterment of ourselves.

Here, I reflect on some of my moments and let you see how they've made me, me. Or, better yet, how I've made myself from them. I'll share a current vision, lay bare my beliefs, and promise to speak from the heart about how I see life. Though, I can't say I have any right answers. This is just one version of the truth I've chosen to live by.

For me, it's essential to allow themes of hope, love, and peace curate my perspectives and understanding of truth. I choose these themes to headline as many moments as I can. They are the bedrock for who I think I should be.

That being said, this book isn't about "how to," or "what you should do." To the contrary, I'm here to ask, "what if?" or "why not?" I don't offer instructions or shortcuts (nor would I be qualified to). I have no plea, no goal of persuasion, or assumption of providence. Instead, I offer you poetry, positivity, and a little provocation.

I can only hope, as I recount times of struggle and growth, days of heartache and joy, or cases of indecisiveness and clarity, that you come to reimagine moments of your own.

Of course, though, we'll define our individual experiences as we see fit. We're each expected to sort out our own moments, like only we can. These pages are dedicated to reflecting on the different ways I've chosen to do so.

By sharing honest reflections, my peak aspiration for *Here We Begin* is to inspire you to characterize your power, encourage you to trust your agency, and help you define, or redefine, your truth. In all, I strive to extend *you* an opportunity to reflect honestly and begin intentionally shaping these moments, for yourself.

Finally, as we move on, I want you to know I'm grateful for this moment, especially. Thank you for the privilege of this time I get to share with you. From here on out, more than ever, we're in this together.

Now, let's begin.

Bring Hope

The Boundless.

May you find peace
in the endless storm.

It will not shrink for you.

May you bound
the boundless,

release all you knew.

May you become greater
beside a greater challenge.

Live your days
with life in the balance.

Correct your mistakes,
when given a chance,

you're more than a mishap
or some circumstance.

May you find solace
and sow hope,

no matter the shape
or how it's grown

or this life
and all you've known.

It's your life.

It's *yours*.

Little Pieces.

There's something so satisfying about life coming together. It's a feeling of release, of freedom. It's like earth is spinning, people around you are moving, car lights glide across late nights, and you can breathe. It gives you permission to move, to expand, to see more, be more. When we perceive something is beginning to fit right, it feels right.

However, when we're so quick to commend ourselves for our accomplishments or the hatching of new and big ideas, we're driven by a conclusion — an end. Sometimes, we forget, and we take for granted the gritty aspects of growth, the incremental feats that truly show us who we are.

We're compromise,

a little now, for the right to hope for more later.

We're a long day-in, for a big night-out.

We're early mornings. We're late nights. We're days in the sun, or days without it. We're long walks, short talks and wholesome conversations. We're moms and dads, sisters and brothers, estranged significant others, and lovers that never were. We're the mini successes, the messes, and all the dumb questions. We're moments with the most important people in our lives, and mistakes that won't cease to be.

That space between our big, seemingly defining moments ought to bear our love.

Imagine, if life were a puzzle, how brilliant, or how beautiful it'd be if we could fall for all the little pieces, all the days you'd wish away if you could?

What if we decided those were the pieces that mattered most and that life's just a little too precious for us to leave any moments in the box?

Maybe,

just maybe,

life can only be as satisfying as each little piece you didn't see,
or think you needed?

Go ahead and place your moments.

I think you'll find a use for each, their purpose fulfilled by your hand.

Greatness.

What if it's not about how much we've accomplished?

What if it's not even about how much we can accomplish?

What if we choose to simply strive toward being the best "me" we can possibly be,

growing, in at least one way, each day?

What if we agree to only let them determine how "successful" we are once it's over?

Not now.
Not before our story's end.

What if there's nothing more ambitious
than committing to a life of greatness

simply, for the sake of greatness…

despite the fact,

choosing faith in yourself
may always be thankless?

The Difference.

You wait forever and a day,

for a day just waiting on you.

You wait.

You bide your time,

"grind and grind,"

at inconsistency.

You wait.

You wait to dream.
You wait to guess.
You wait to believe
You wait to test.
You wait to cry.
You wait to go.
You wait to try.
You wait to know.

You wait for a smile.
You wait in shame.

You wait for denial.
You wait in pain.

You wait in wait.

What if I told you,
you can't out-wait, fate.

Still, though the time goes,

here you are.

You wait with the flow.

You've waited too long,
to move, or to grow.

It's just the difference between

a yes or a no,

 a "Sure, I'll go!"

or,

 a "no, I won't."

Passion.

The ache in your muscles,
you wouldn't know
how to move without it.

Where it doesn't matter
how far you've come.

That deep feeling
in the pit of your stomach,

a place you go,
where you hide

the butterflies,
the fear ridden times,
the tired pride,

all beside

a hope

you can't deny.

Still,

it feels like
one gut-punch away
from spilling it all.

In the Eyes.

Look them in the eyes
when they tell you, "no."

Look them in the eyes
and see how many times
someone said it to them.

Their dream deferred,
the color of the iris,

surely you can tell
they were denied it.

It's clear as day.

Unable to master their own fate

so they find a way
to shackle yours,

and you let them.

With your head down,
eyes to the ground,
some melancholy frown…

It won't do.

If they couldn't beat them,
they can't defeat you.

You're showing your hand

in how you hold your head,
you can choose a different view.

look up, instead.

In a quiet moment between words
you can see their self-reflection.

You realize
this isn't the life
they would've chosen

if they could do it again.

Ambition.

Ambition is more
than climbing an ivory tower.

It lives in us all.

It's okay to be empowered.

True to size,
she cannot hide,

she cannot be disguised.

Leave her out

where everyone can see her,
where everyone can hear her,
you know they'll move,
just to be near her.

It's not about being the overachiever.

It's not about being something
or someone you're not.

Instead, be the best something
or someone you could be.

"Three things you're grateful for — go!"

(I won't be offended if you take time to write them in)

Libra.

In search of myself,
I've found one thing clear:

life's in the balance,
we're living this moment,

though another is near.

Today,

I'm the best writer
I've ever been.

Nevertheless,

my best
will forever be fleeting.

Tomorrow,

I'll be the best writer
I've ever been.

There is no sense now
in repeating.

I'll write of today,

but not the next page, too.

A new day means

I'll be written anew.

The Place.

It's a place of quiet thoughts and learned behaviors.

It's a place where passion and pride breathe new air
over your cool fire.

It's there that brings me hope when there needn't be, assumes my fate is what I make of it

— day by day, choice by choice —

only what I take of it.

It's that which holds together what would otherwise cease to be, what would otherwise dream of being.

Here, will never let me forget from who, or from where, I came…

Where I started believing.

Not where the heart is,

but where it braves to remember why.

Or better yet,

why not?

Everyone has such a place.

To Find Us.

I don't think it matters

when you get back up

if you don't know why.

Or, that,
at the end of the day,

indifference

or complacency

can have its stay.

You have to give way
to a belief,

something in which you can be found.

***

I know nowadays,

nightmares range

from wake to woke
from I'm right, you're wrong

to, "I told you so."

But, if we wake today,
this world is ours.

If these thoughts of mine
yell louder and louder
and your hand waits patiently still,

the space between my fingertips
no longer wanting,

waning to be filled…

If this soul longs

to confide in another
and that other is you,

it's no matter who you were before,
I've struggled too.

There can be so much more,
when we're here for each other

and when there's hope to go 'round.

In that, I can believe.

In that, we can be found.

A Friend.

I want you to know,
it's okay to eat alone.

It's okay to work-out alone,
read alone,
go on adventures alone —

need to be alone.

Struggle alone if you must.

But, now that we're here,

you don't *have* to.

You can rely on me.

I'm not going
anywhere.

If it gets to be a burden to bear

"I'll be
right there,"

beside you.

Enough, Yet.

An indomitable will
comes with a bleeding heart,

the morning after,
the day before,

cold feet,
wounded deep,

lonely days,
lonelier nights...

Head held high,

you chose this life —
and what a gift that is.

You'd rather dream,
you'd rather fail.

***

Maybe, the most courageous we can ever be, is looking at our lives with optimism, fighting the urge to quit or settle for something less than we worked for, less than we dreamt for — hurt for.

Courage is waking up in the morning, every morning, and choosing to try when an achy heart pleads desperately, whispers softly, or forgets the,

"why"

In its purest form, true courage belongs to those who dare to hope
beyond the fear of pain, or failure —

to those who refuse to believe in the notion
they're not enough,

but instead,
they're not enough,

yet.

Swim.

The world makes its point
one way
or another.

Try as you might,
carefully, wishfully,

we're not meant to
go blissfully,

pain free.

It's the way of the world.

It ebbs
to deal a blow.

and so,

you can choose to be whisked,
and warped in the flow

or, swim.

Winning.

It's not your fault,

from the beginning,
they told you it was all about winning.

Maybe, they were right,
despite the fact you can't always be —

"that."

It's not about being on top at all times,

running the world,

trying, lying,
grinding at the wrong rock,
barking up the wrong tree,

all the while,
dying
at the stake of their expectations.

What if nobody wanted more for you, than you?

What if, even though they taught you to be this,

you'd rather be the best that —

that, which only you could be.

What if you gave yourself your all,

became something they've never seen?

Not out of spite,

just out to inspire.

Don't be mistaken,
hard work is dire,

but it's a choice we all make.

This could be your victory.
This can be your empire.

They told you from the beginning
it was all about winning,

and they were right.

My Stars.

Not a night goes by

where I don't wish on my stars.

Sometimes, I think,

they can't be that far…

When in denial,
I'll wander a while,

but always bring hope

I'll let the world drift away,
and reach them, someday…

Believe.

You are a dream
worth waiting for.

One day (at a time).

Just one day closer

to that "one day" life.

One day closer

to that sincere
and deep sigh,

for all I've done,
to stand right with pride,

how far we've come.

Dauntless, we defeated
the ravenous tide.

***

We may just be
one day closer now,

but I really believe

what you give
is what you get,

and conviction
is all we'll need.

Until these thankless days have gone,

just one day closer,

is just our "one day," won...

Know Love

Where the "It" Lies.

This morning, I saw the "It,"

been looking all my life.

I was born of "It,"
in a town that fit
the grip of my palm.

Heard it once,
before the bus in first grade,

needed to get on,
and make someone's day,

looked back to the flag
and, "remember what I say."

I felt it once in my mom's embrace,

tears down her shoulder,

a lake, where I buried my face,

she'd never let me go,
just move at my pace.

I touched it once,
for only a second,

and, I'll always remember,
it was me who wrecked it.

I'm moved by "It,"

motivated by it,

everything I need,
everything I fought for,
everything inside my core,
and then some.

"It" moves in silence,
and rarely speaks loud.

But, when it does,

to "It," we're all bound.

I saw the "It" this morning,

let it warm me,
let it still my breath,
let it coax my words
until I had none left.

I saw the "It" this morning,

in a new,
unique hue,

what a pretty shade.
what a lovely view.

Grateful.

Where goofy meets grateful,
lighthearted means falling hard,

falling in the way
I always hoped to,

I don't have to think
when I'm with you.

I guess that's why
I make you laugh so much.

I don't have to think
when I'm with you,

and that's made all the difference.

I guess that's why
you make me laugh so much.

The One.

But, you have to know

what you're passionate about

before you can know

who you're passionate about.

Her Spirit.

I don't fear the fight for you.

I fear the battle won.

To usher you here,
I must refuse.

I won't be party
to an empty morning,
some want for more,

or polish your heart
like a porcelain chore.

I cannot watch such a will
become a ghost in this life —

let you be simple, steady,
and unfulfilled,

a spirit in the night.

If I'm not enough,

who am I
to speak of me any differently
on your behalf?

If I'm not what you need,

I'm no less a man,
and what we had
was no less real.

Soothed by morning,

brighter days await us both.

Clarity's for you now,
I have all I need.

This — all of this,

is all it could be.

She was first.

When I was young
I was certain
I'd see you again.

Like a strand of destiny,
gone astray,

I set life's course,
preparing for that day.

But now, I'm unsure.

I realize,
that long ago,
I gave your feelings
to the earth.

Thus,
despite many years
and all I've grown,

the fleeting trends,
fair-weather friends,
and bleeding hearts,

I'll never get to show,

and you'll never have to know.

So…

I suppose,

in light of this path
I once thought *you* chose,

I loved you just enough

to learn how
to show myself
to love myself.

Who I am,
is just who I am,
without you

not despite you,

surely made better
by all you are to me.

What a Man Can Be.

A man is strong,
like his heart,

only wise,
when patience allows.

A man is brave,

a ferocious idea,

with compassion endowed.

A man is much more
than some story of himself,

when, with the people he needs,

he treads light
and takes count.

He is brave,

a ferocious idea,

and if that idea
were such as love?

Love that he feels
even though it's tough.

Maybe then may a man
find real peace enough.

Yearning Thunder.

Holding my breath,
afraid you'll set my world on fire.

The view might change,
but my feelings don't.

This night might end,
but I plea it won't.

Where lightning breaks the sky, that's where you'll find me.

Where minutes turn to hours,
I'd watch time expand,

see the slow-motion version
of all I love, everything you do.

Perilous clouds
prelude our symphony.

Where lightning breaks the sky, that's where you'll find me.

Know this,
I'm but a moment behind,

waiting, wanting, wooing
your sudden flash of light.

You are truly, one of a kind.

I'm here,
I'm yours,
though, surely, you're free…

Where lightning breaks the sky, that's where you'll find me.

A Long Night.

If a clock keeps ticking,
I'll lose my mind.

Too late to move.
Too late tonight.

My heart,
a loathing entity,

I long for sleep,
I need serenity.

In a moment of vigor,
I see your face.

Bold enough to miss you.
Brave enough to choose to.

Dare I say,
this needn't drag on.

Blue eyes await me,
your warmth is the dawn

and yet, I lay here,
under sleepless stars

aimlessly pleading

morning, and you,
not be too far.

Thankfully,

a clock still ticks.

Aeronauts.

Am I enough for her?
Will I be all she needs?
What, from me, is she hoping to see?

I need her already.

What should I say?
Will she lead me astray?
How can I know?

Can she find herself
in the way I stride?
In the way I walk
right by her side?

What if we rely on each other?

Fight every day,
would we duck,
run for cover?

What if we grow too fast?
Will she wither away,
Work harder to stay?
Will she have patience to wait?

Could I even ask her to?
Would I even have to?

Maybe we're cursed,
our aspirations coming first,
do we let things burst?

Could I convince you otherwise?
Would I even have to?

As we ascend
into the atmosphere
and find ourselves alone,
our inhibitions overthrown,
disenchanted with
the brick,
the stick,
and the stone…
will we have enough courage
to outlast
the unknown?

"Three things you love about *yourself* — Go!"

True Love.

To wonder
is to breathe.

To believe
is to best fear.

To want for more
is to be grateful.

To lift others
is to lift oneself.

But, to love…

To love
is to long

for the best version of yourself,

flaws and all.

She Snores.

Trapped under the comforter,
even though it's not comfortable,

but I'm comforted
by how comfy she looks.

Tonight, she's out,
even though her mind is loud,

and I strain myself,
tuning into each sound,

just a little bit fragile,
this lovely heart I've found.

I've found a little more of myself uncovered, under these covers and I'm not sure whether I can share it with others. I mean, she's safe. I don't know how that makes me feel. Family is safe. But, like my mother with my brothers, I find myself frustrated.

Like, how many times do I have to say
I want what's best for you?

Though, what if she really *does* do better than me?

What if she leaves,
and all I'm left with is envy?

Maybe, she's a little too close, I mean, it's warm under these sheets and I'm sweating. Or, maybe, that's just me realizing how vulnerable I am and how that never happens with anybody... not like this. I kind of wish she'd keep snoring like that, ignore me, be a brat, give me a reason to pack up, leave fast. But she won't, and I can't.

This is where I am,
and frankly,
I'm a fan

of how she snores.

The Comet.

I picture rolling over
into the Milky Way,

falling…

falling further and deeper
than anyone ever has before.

I imagine what it'd be like
to be an astronaut,
exploring the untold,
unseen nature of my universe…

it's darkest corners,
it's craziest secrets.

I think about what it would be like
to see the day and night
in their purest form,

see stars
explode, reform,
like cosmic cognition,

to see the infinite possibilities
beyond everything we know.

I imagine my descent…

falling out of control
without fear or reserve,

open to the light,
the dark,

the red, purple, orange and yellow — the blue.

Celestial beauty, possibility…

and intertwined, cradled, and refined,

I feel love.

Something so abstract and surreal,

the deeper I fall,
the more it feels real.

It cascades down upon me
through me,
within me
until it is me…

and… for the first time… the very first time,
I have all I need…

I have all I need.

Here, in space,
time will unwind

so I can unbind

the very confines of this universe.

Yes, I'm finally

me.

I picture rolling over… rolling over into you, and reflected so perfectly in your eyes there I am. I'm here for you. Witness and welcome to the unraveling of the unfamiliar, a pioneer of the greatest, most mysterious galaxy known to man.

Thus, all at once,
I'm part of a new plan.

I'm finally acquainted
with my universe.

Sunday Afternoon.

If I lay here any longer,
I'll forget to get up,
I'll forget to face the day.

If I lay here any longer,
I might find peace.

Not one piece of me
left in the fray
left to overlay,

like we do.

If I lay here any longer,
I'll forget what it means
to breathe my own air.

But, somehow,
the feeling of last night
and starlight

still feels right

and I don't wanna go.

I don't wanna go.

Honestly.

I love you

even when you don't know
you love me back —

I don't need you to.

Honestly,

I decided I would

from the moment I could.

Whether you like it or not,

here I am.

A friend,
to pretend
but, still,

here I am.

In Color.

Life, is lived in shades,

a color for each of us,
a palette that plays
with abstract patterns

pressed against
who we'd like to be.

I've seen in many colors,

like new lenses,

a worldview
that paints my days
the color of my ways,

holds my hopes

until my dreams come-true,

one shout-to-the-stars at a time.

What we have, is what we have.

How we get there —
who we get there with,

determines its color,

or, at least,
it's vibrancy.

***

People, choices, passion, hope, justice, truth,

and forgiveness.

Fear, power, prayer,

gratuity, humility —

her heart,

my mind,

your pain,

our dreams…

These are the colors I see.

These are the colors we bleed,
unto the world

I choose to love.

The Lines.

Read between the lines,

plead between the taught lines
around the subtle outlines of her skin

and when she wakes you
let her in.

Let her spirit haze you.

She needn't praise you.

Just rest beneath this crystal shine
embedded in the sky

For we're all stuck between
these lines we read,

the blind
leading the blind
across tonight's lonely lie.

But, where else
might I have this chance

to follow you
in, or outside
the lines?

Disarmed.

No anger,
or pain.

No revolt,
or frustration

in my veins.

Just me,
vulnerable, torn.

Nothing else
worth looking for,

and
the air
has escaped
the prison
of my lungs.

There's no moisture left
here on my tongue,

ears rung,

simply overcome —

by her smile.

A Moment with You.

A moment with you speaks for itself,
but we talk a little louder,

so I don't look weird
staring at you.

A moment with you is brash,
like waves on rocks in the storm.

When I look in your eyes,
I'm on the seashore,

and you know
I love the sea.

This moment —
steady, and in focus

Of course,
you already know this

but, in a moment with you

I'm here,
I can stay
I can wait for tomorrow,
I can live 'till I'm gray.

Tell me about it,

I see the strain,
don't hesitate,

to say my name…

No,

a moment with you is slow,
but never idle,

side by side,
we'll keep our lives
on bedside

while you're listening to my heartbeat.

Believe it all —

I've seen it all,

all in a moment, with you.

Her Name.

I know why you run from her,

man, I know the truth,

I've been there,
I've felt it too.

It took one goofy hi,
and you knew,

no matter how far you ran,
or what you'd say,
or what you'd do,

she would always have some part of you.

You'll hand it to her,
or she'll just break you in two —

that, at least,
you can choose.

But this is simple,

she got the best of you.

I promise it's okay.
I promise you'll be better for it.
I promise you some pain,

but you'll have joy, too.

I promise you so much joy.

Let that be her name.

You're Wanted.

I hope you choose people
who choose you.

Go where you're wanted,
where you can be whole
and still be held.

When it comes to hearts,
I hope you choose theirs,

and there's never a doubt,

you're the one
they can't go without —

you're the one
they won't leave behind.

Go there,
you've seen it,

where your care is greeted,
where you're believed in

There is clarity there.

There is trust there.

There is real love there —

and it will make the difference.

Value Peace

Where I Come From.

I come from a one stoplight town,
from Memorial Park,

basketball,
and brothers.

I come from black,

I come from white,

I come from what's between
the lines.

I come from talks with mom,
and my dad's sacrifice.

I come from the house on a hill,
from, "did you make someone's day."

I come from hard work,
encouragement,
from, "do it the right way."

I come from hope,

I come from love,
and the pursuit of happiness.

I come from progress.

I am progress.

What Do You Value?

Who we are

can be
whomever we choose

beyond

what we're doing,
who we're with, or
where we are now —

when we're loyal to

what we value.

Thoughts and Prayers.

Alas, suspended upon the platitudes
of these people and this place,

I remain aloft,

strung out on words
I've surely heard
over and over,

as if they're enough.

Voices
in my mind
say all there is to say.

Voices,
not all kind,

say all there is these days.

So, I'm moved
this way and that,

drifting, sifting
through a sea of words.

As they move around me,
surround me,
bury me,

make it harder
and harder

to spot
the righteous shore,
it's harder to see…

All these voices,

all so lonely.

I'm tired,

tired of the screaming,
shrieking,
crying
for someone,
anyone,
to please act.

please,
just act.

Just say something.

So much violence.

So much pain,

in this world

simply a product
of things
left unsaid.

Withered.

Inevitably, we stalk the best version of ourselves.

Whether we confess to it
or not,
it's who we are

to dream of who we could,
should,
or would be.

We're all dependent
on a life of growth.

Without it,
righteous pain
sprouts mangled,

untenable
in its place.

It's pain that's quick
to know nothing
but absence of care,

next, it'll be, "well that's not fair."

It'll take
what's not given

to endear some faux survival.

Gripping at others,
it will coil itself,

hoping for revival.

An icky pain,
misunderstood.

An icky pain,

we'd spare
if we could.

Lonely, untillable,

in a barren place,

no light to lean,
little hope to glean,

a dark place
we cannot to see,

where dreams of others
must die, too.

Deep down you know,
this shouldn't be you,

it's not
who you were meant to be.

My Friend.

Miss the people
who will *see* you do well.

Mind the people
who will *help* you do well,

the ones not afraid

to get their hands dirty
holding you accountable,

the ones who show you valor,

who will lend you courage

when the world asks you to forget.

Purpose.

Some days,
It's hard remembering
to what guise
I owe my morning,

to what cause
I owe my life.

When my last day comes,

I'm right with hope,

I may live on
in the hearts
I touch in kind

wherever I go…

to you I must yield
my most passionate soul,

of which my time —
of which each day —

of which each moment

I'll always owe.

Envy.

We all seek to do beautiful things
of one word or another.

But, as they say,
beauty rests in the fickle eye
of her beholder.

We all seek to do beautiful things,

our lowly task,
our subtle obsession
our quiet devotion,

a most painful,
universal,
but valuable lesson.

We all seek to do beautiful things.

We all seem to do beautiful things.

Would you fall with grace?

Though your name wasn't called,
did you lend love
hate's hiding place?

Where spite seeks to build a home,
did you address your neighbor?

Offer your labor?

Come, when asked a favor?

Behold, the fury
you can hardly confide.

When they bludgeoned you with reckless belief,

wanton disregard
for the pain you hide
and the dreams you seek,

the deepest weight you keep —
destined you beneath,

rarely do we think to ask,

"why?"

Or wonder, if it were you,

"would I?"

Carelessly, zealously,
unsparingly,
we rumble merrily

As if their pain

is easy to ignore.

It's easy to forget
who forgiveness is for…

who patience

and engagements,

civil,
thoughtful,
multi-perspective,
respectful conversations
and statements are for.

But here you are
trying to be the just-one.

But, it's so much bigger than just how you feel…

Would you fall with grace?

Lead yourself to leap
and look truth in the face.

As we demand days of peace,

do we know what these words mean?

Ask yourself,
just in case.

What is a leader
without humility?

What is humanity
but generosity?

What is peace,
if not hope?
without love?

Privilege.

To wait,
to take each moment
like it's not your last,
or your only.

To breathe,
but not gasp,

To defer,
do what you prefer.

To take it in from the sidelines.

To waste the day,
or any day,

to roll out of bed,
pour a cup of coffee,
read the news,
watch cartoons,
go back to sleep,
even 'till noon,

like,

"I'll get up soon."

to wait for the right time
to think up the right line
or phrase,

to know how to shake hands
the right way,
or say,

"meh, today, just wasn't my day…"

Because, you'll probably have another chance.

To sabotage,
distract, redact,

choose not to act,

distort the facts,
be calm, be loud,
be *too proud,*
be slow, be fast,

or be dead last.

be late, hesitate,
pontificate,
be in control

of my own fate,

and laugh it off…

to choose,
to be,
to just do me…

My privilege.

Just Us.

If I hear the cries
behind your eyes

see the doubt
in your smile,

your hate,
doused in style,

are you still alone?

Am I?

If you can hear my heartbeat,
can't you hear theirs too?

Would it be too great a rouse
to walk in their shoes?
… if you really wanted to?

In a true test of fate,
could I bare my soul to you?

What care would you take?

I'll tell you the truth,

I'll only give mercy
for whatever you'd do.

I'll give you my hope,
I'll give you my love,
I'll give you patience
kindness, respect —

all the above.

Not because I'm weak
and not because I must,

because at the end of the day —
its really just us.

Empathy.

I can see you,

because I'm looking,
listening.

I can see you,
now's your chance,

say something.

Show me what you need us to know,
or don't.

I will be here
just the same.

Any Change?

I'm sorry, I don't have any.

I'm sorry sir, I'm out.

Ma'am, I'm sorry…
God bless you.

I don't have any
but, wow…

I'm sorry they took your home,

I'm sorry you have to roam.

I'm sorry they didn't hear you cry
over car horns
and cell phones.

I'm sorry they stole from you
and never gave you a chance.

I'm sorry who you are,
only warrants a glance.

I'm sorry they shudder
when they walk your way.

I'm sorry for everything
they were supposed to say.

I'm sorry for the nights
you spend hiding from the rain.

I'm sorry they treat you
like some kind of strain,

like some kind of stain

on these littered streets.

I'm sorry this world
wasn't made to suit you,

won't care,
lend a prayer
or a decent pair of shoes

but, often,
they'll try and forget about you…

I'm sorry,
I really have nothing to share

no minute to spare,
no second glance,
no bus fare

no praise,
no rage,
no change these days.

I'm sorry,

If only I knew
I have more than enough.

The Example.

Maybe, our righteousness unsoftened by humility is at fault.

They might not be right to believe how they do,

but who are we to reciprocate their hate with hate?

It doesn't mean your pain, or frustration, or rage ought to disappear... or even could.

Instead, it means that we're being called to meet this moment,
as we are.

It means that many of us are going to face this moment...
broken.

But, to you I say:

what if there's no other way?

What if, at the end of the day, the change you seek rests on the other side of your pain?

What if the hardest thing — harder than the spirited debates, the rallies, the name calling, the divisiveness — is understanding...

is choosing to seek humanity
in any place, no matter how dim.

Hateful or hopeful,
life goes on.

The direction we need to take demands more than righteousness can afford.

It's not enough.

Progress demands our empathy, an unprecedented degree of love and hope from each and every one of us.

It's no longer enough to be right.

It's about healing our wounds,

bringing together worlds of people that,
although they don't know it yet,

are *crying out loud* to shed the awful burdens given to them
before they knew how, or why.

In other words,
as they say —

it's time to embody the change
you want to see in others.

It's time to lead.

It's time to be an example of the world

we wish to see.

The Role Model.

They'll never know the ache of a crisp morning.

They're as deep in the dark as you are,

walking these sidewalks,
whispering to the wind
like an only friend,

wondering if
you'll ever get to sleep again.

They'll never know
the nights,

wanting pain from the day
to drift away
only to get back to work.

It hurts.

They can't possibly know
days worth crying a lot,

or recall
days worth lying about.

They might not understand you,
want the most, or the best for you,

the way you do…

But you can,
and you will,

so that, one day,
they'll see how

they can too.

For Peace.

Great leaders are not concerned with whether or not people believe in them,

only whether or not people believe in themselves.

Great leaders, with their honesty, humanity, and heart

show just how easy it can be

to make a difference.

Great leaders, above all,

know the true price of peace —

humility.

Believe.

Sometimes, it's all you can do
to let the night
pour tears of moonlight
down your face.

When you look to the sky
do you let it define you?

Is all that's before you
here to deride you?

Inside you,
beside you,
love has its way,

let the breath you breathe for others,
the patience you give your brothers,
the moments you spend
mending those who suffer

guide you,

it's all equal
to the love you'll take…

where karma around the corner
lends discretion to the mind,

where the one they see
matches the who inside,

where what you've written in stone
transcends the divide,

believe in all you've done…

when dimming sunlight,
turns water to amber wine,

when you find the right place
to free your mind,

when your heart finally finds one
and the soul agrees —

some nights may pour you
moonlight tears.

Fear not,
you've come so far

smile, triumph,
you've made it.

you're *here*.

Here, We Begin.

Across the fault lines of our hearts,

the dog days,
the it's too far days,
the see these scars days,

they're no more.

No, we haven't forgotten,

We've chosen to forgive.

We did that.

Up against the odds,
and all they've done,
we've moved in inches
and taken a mile.

We've lasted merely seconds,
but weathered a great storm.

Day-by-day,
way-by-way,
we've found our grace.

We've found our direction amid their sleepless taunts and hollowed glory.

To them we say at last:

Here, today, on this day, I'm no more of what you've made me — on this day, I'm more than the mirror, more than spite, more than your wickedness and a complacent life. Here, today, on this day, I'm all I've been, but not all I'm yet to be. Watch me move, watch me work, watch me stay my hand, watch me love void of jealousy.

Watch me grow where you said there wasn't room,
Watch me own these scars you've sown.

Watch me.
Watch and you'll see.

Yes, today, on this day, I'm made by my hand. I'll take responsibility for what's passed and what's yet to come. I'll talk with my failure, take pride in my success. I'll build with these hands but know when to rest. I'll heal with this heart, let it beat from my chest.

I'll recast my destiny, believe in what's true.

I'm more than I know and beyond what you knew.

Here, today — on this day — I'm free.

Yes, right here,
I'm becoming whoever I want to be...

Here, we begin

to dream bigger than before,

it's not about then.

it's about now.

it's not about when.

it's about how.

Here, we're not reborn or reformed.

We're realigned,

repurposed —
redefined.

Here,

we bring hope,
we know love,
we value peace.

Here, we begin.

Made in the USA
Monee, IL
14 July 2020